# UKRAINE

R.L. Van

Big Buddy Books
An Imprint of Abdo Publishing
abdobooks.com

**abdobooks.com**

Published by Abdo Publishing, a division of ABDO, PO Box 398166, Minneapolis, Minnesota 55439.
Copyright © 2023 by Abdo Consulting Group, Inc. International copyrights reserved in all countries. No part of this book may be reproduced in any form without written permission from the publisher. Big Buddy Books™ is a trademark and logo of Abdo Publishing.

Printed in the United States of America, North Mankato, Minnesota
102022
012023

Design: Emily O'Malley, Mighty Media, Inc.
Production: Mighty Media, Inc.
Editor: Jessica Rusick
Cover Photograph: Sodel Vladyslav/Shutterstock Images
Interior Photographs: Alexander Wienerberger/Wikimedia Commons, p. 28 (bottom right); Andrew Angelov/
    Shutterstock Images, p. 30 (currency); Andrey Zhernovoy/Shutterstock Images, p. 6 (bottom); Anton_
    Ivanov/Shutterstock Images, p. 26 (right); Belikova Oksana/Shutterstock Images, p. 27 (top left); byvalet/
    Shutterstock Images, p. 26 (left); Dmytro Larin/Shutterstock Images, p. 23; Drop of Light/Shutterstock
    Images, p. 29 (bottom); Ekaterina Chesnokova/AP Images, p. 21; Fotokon/Shutterstock Images, p. 28
    (bottom left); Ingus Kruklitis/Shutterstock Images, p. 6 (top); JaySi/Shutterstock Images, p. 15; Khuntul laut/
    Shutterstock Images, p. 7 (map); konstantinks/Shutterstock Images, p. 30 (flag); krolya25/Shutterstock
    Images, p. 27 (bottom); lukulo/iStockphoto, pp. 5 (compass), 7 (compass); lux3000/Shutterstock Images,
    p. 29 (top); meunierd/Shutterstock Images, p. 9; New Africa/Shutterstock Images, p. 13; Pyty/Shutterstock
    Images, p. 5 (world map); Rosliak Nataliia/Shutterstock Images, p. 25; Ruslan Kalnitsky/Shutterstock
    Images, p. 27 (top right); Ryzhkov Oleksandr/Shutterstock Images, p. 17; Sergiy Bykhunenko/Shutterstock
    Images, p. 6 (middle); Timolina/Shutterstock Images, p. 19; Yuri Ivanov/AP Images, p. 11
Design Elements: Mighty Media, Inc.
Country population and area figures taken from the CIA World Factbook

Library of Congress Control Number: 2022940505

**Publisher's Cataloging-in-Publication Data**
Names: Van, R.L., author.
Title: Ukraine / by R.L. Van
Description: Minneapolis, Minnesota : Abdo Publishing, 2023 | Series: Countries | Includes online resources and index.
Identifiers: ISBN 9781532199752 (lib. bdg.) | ISBN 9781098274955 (ebook)
Subjects: LCSH: Ukraine--Juvenile literature. | Europe--Juvenile literature. | Ukraine--History--Juvenile literature. | Geography--Juvenile literature.
Classification: DDC 947.7--dc23

# CONTENTS

# PASSPORT TO UKRAINE

Ukraine is a country in eastern Europe. It borders seven other countries, the Black Sea, and the Sea of Azov. More than 43 million people live there.

WHERE IS UKRAINE?

N
W
E
S
Belarus
Russia
Poland
UKRAINE
Slovakia
Hungary
Romania
Moldova
Sea of
Azov
Black Sea

# IMPORTANT CITIES

Kyiv is Ukraine's **capital** and largest city. It is a center of business, education, and culture.

Kharkiv is Ukraine's second-largest city. It is a modern city known for its unique architecture.

Odesa is Ukraine's third-largest city. It is a historic port city on the Black Sea. It is known for its beaches.

## SAY IT

**Kyiv**
*KEEV*

**Kharkiv**
*HAHR-keev*

**Odesa**
*oh-DEH-suh*

## DID YOU KNOW?

Kharkiv was the **capital** of Ukraine from 1919 to 1934.

# UKRAINE IN HISTORY

People have lived in Ukraine for thousands of years. Many groups have fought to control the land. Over the years, Russia, Lithuania, Poland, and Austria have all controlled parts of Ukraine. By 1922, Ukraine was part of the **Soviet Union**.

Saint Olga of Kyiv (*center*) ruled parts of Ukraine in the 900s.

Joseph Stalin was a **dictator** of the **Soviet Union**. Millions of Ukrainians died during his rule. During **World War II**, Germany attacked Ukraine. Millions of Ukrainians were killed. In 1991, the Soviet Union ended. Ukraine became independent. However, it has struggled with **corruption** and conflict with Russia.

Leaders from Russia, Belarus, and Ukraine signed the Belovezh Accords to end the Soviet Union.

# AN IMPORTANT SYMBOL

Ukraine's flag is blue and yellow. The colors represent blue skies over fields of wheat.

Ukraine is a **semi-presidential republic**. The president is head of state. The prime minister is head of government. Parliament makes laws.

Ukraine adopted its flag in 1992.

# ACROSS THE LAND

Most of Ukraine is flat grassland called steppe. The country has highlands, lowlands, and mountains.

Wolves, deer, bears, polecats, storks, and grouse live in Ukraine. Mushrooms, pine trees, oak trees, and grasses grow there.

The Dnieper River is the longest river in Ukraine and the fourth-longest in Europe.

# EARNING A LIVING

Ukraine's factory workers make food products, metals, and trains. Many people work in service jobs, such as banking or teaching.

Ukraine's **natural resources** include iron ore, coal, and oil. Farmers produce wheat, potatoes, sugar beets, fruits, and milk.

Ukraine is often called
the "breadbasket of
Europe." Wheat is an
important crop there.

# LIFE IN UKRAINE

Many Ukrainians live in cities. They eat bread, potatoes, beets, and mushrooms. Soups, dumplings, and cabbage rolls are popular dishes.

In Ukraine, soccer, boxing, basketball, and ice hockey are favorite sports. Many Ukrainians are **Eastern Orthodox** Christians.

Borscht, or beet soup, is popular in Ukraine. It can be eaten hot or cold.

# 8

# FAMOUS FACES

Ani Lorak was born in Kitsman, Ukraine. She became famous on a children's music TV show as a teen. In 2008, she won second place in the Eurovision Song Contest. She was later named the People's Artist of Ukraine.

Ani Lorak's real name is
Karolina. "Ani Lorak" is
Karolina spelled backward.

Volodymyr Zelenskyy was born in Kryvyi Rih, Ukraine. After earning a law degree, he became a comedian and actor. He also spoke out against **corruption** in government. Zelenskyy was elected president of Ukraine in 2019. He was celebrated for his leadership when Russia invaded Ukraine in 2022.

Volodymyr Zelenskyy called on foreign countries to aid Ukraine during the Russian invasion.

# 9

# A GREAT COUNTRY

Ukraine has beautiful land and a rich history and culture. The people and places of Ukraine help make the world a more interesting place.

**DID YOU KNOW?**

Ukraine's national flower is the sunflower.

Hoverla is the highest
peak in Ukraine. It is a
popular place to hike.

# TOUR BOOK

If you ever visit Ukraine, here are some places to go and things to do!

## IMAGINE

See a show at one of Ukraine's puppet theaters. The Kyiv Academic Puppet Theater is the oldest in the country.

## REMEMBER

The National Chernobyl Museum holds a collection of items related to the accidental **nuclear** explosion.

## DISCOVER

Visit Lemurian Lake. Algae gives the water its pink color.

## LEARN

Visit the National Museum of Folk Architecture and Life of Ukraine to learn about Ukraine's history.

## EAT

Lviv is known for its chocolate. At Lviv Chocolate Factory, you can watch the chocolates being made and sample some sweets!

# TIMELINE

## 800s

Kyivan Rus was established. It was an important state that covered Ukraine, Belarus, and parts of Russia.

## MID-1200s

The king of Rus founded the first city in what is now Ukraine.

## 1918

Ukraine declared independence from Russia. In 1922, Ukraine became part of the **Soviet Union**.

## 1932–1933

Millions of Ukrainian people died under Joseph Stalin's rule.

## 1986

The Chernobyl **nuclear** power station exploded. People, animals, and land were badly hurt.

## 2014

Russia began the Russo-Ukrainian War and claimed areas of Ukraine.

## 2022

Russia invaded Ukraine. It claimed that Ukraine should be part of Russia. Millions of **refugees** fled Ukraine.

# UKRAINE
## UP CLOSE

**Official Name**
Ukrayina (Ukraine)

**Flag**

**Population**
43,528,136 (2022 est.)
35th-most-populated country

**Total Area**
233,032 square miles
(603,550 sq km)
45th-largest country

**Official Language**
Ukrainian

**Capital**
Kyiv

**Currency**
Ukrainian hryvnia

**Form of Government**
Semi-presidential
republic

**National Anthem**
"Shche ne vmerla
Ukraina" ("Ukraine
Has Not Yet
Perished")

# GLOSSARY

**capital**—a city where government leaders meet.

**corruption**—dishonest or illegal behaviors done by people in power for personal gain.

**dictator**—a ruler with complete control who often governs in a cruel way.

**Eastern Orthodox**—a Christian church with many followers in eastern Europe. Its followers believe in saints and have special traditions of worship.

**natural resources**—useful and valuable supplies from nature.

**nuclear**—a type of energy that uses atoms. It can cause dangerous explosions and effects.

**refugees**—people leaving an area where there is violence to find safety.

**semi-presidential republic**—a form of government in which an elected president shares power with a prime minister and an elected legislature.

**Soviet Union**—the first country to form a government based on the system known as Communism. It existed from 1922 to 1991.

**World War II**—a war fought in Europe, Asia, and Africa from 1939 to 1945.

# ONLINE RESOURCES

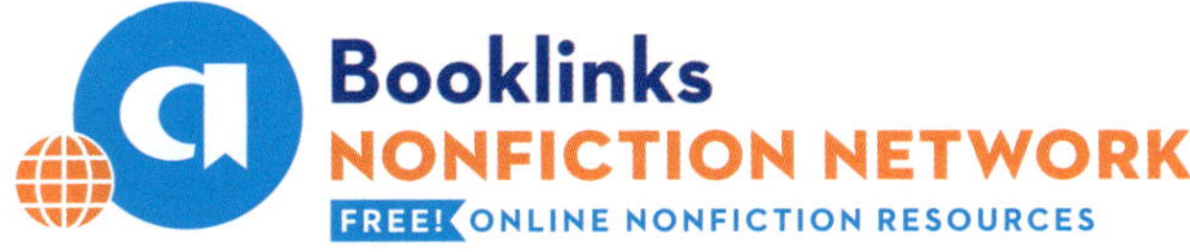

To learn more about Ukraine, please visit **abdobooklinks.com** or scan this QR code. These links are routinely monitored and updated to provide the most current information available.

# INDEX